A BURNING DESIRE

Whit Deschner

The Eddie Tern Press

Atlantis - El Dorado - Camelot - Vallhalla - Shangra La - Freeloadia - Baker City

Other books by Whit Deschner

Does the Wet Suit You? The Confessions of a Kayak Bum*
Burning the Iceberg The Alaskan Fisherman's Novel
How to Be a Jerk in Bristol Bay*
Travels With a Kayak
Lapses in Synapsis
The Early Word Gets the Burn   Short Stories

Gliding into Trouble: The Accounts of Four Student Glider Pilots
by Tom Deschner; Foreword and Edited by Whit Deschner

We Will Not Cease The New Zealand Classic
by Archibald Baxter, North American edition; Edited by Whit Deschner

*Out of print

For pricing and more information go to: whitdeschner.com, or write:

The Eddie Tern Press
1640 3rd St
Baker City, OR 97814
USA

deschnerwhit@yahoo.com

DEDICATED TO MARK HASLETT
(AKA "BEAN SPROUT")

PREFACE

Years ago, I had the audacity to send a batch of my poems to Willard Espy, Wil-liam Rosa Cole and later, Baxter Black.

Willard Espy, famed Philologist and nonsense word collector wrote:

> *"'I had great fun reading your verses. Some work out beautifully. My own instinct would be to shine some of them up a little; the right buffing and they would gleam."*

Unfortunately, I never asked him which ones were gleamers in need of a buff before he passed.

William Rosa Cole, another light verse heavy, who is best known for *The Oxford Book of American Light Verse* wrote:

> *"They're good, most of 'em. Some I'd like to use in an anthology."*

But before he got to publish another anthology, he too, passed.

Some years later, at the National Cowboy Poetry Gathering in Elko Nevada, where I was explaining to a bunch of inebriated cowboys my animal-licked salt licks as art auctioned off for charity, I met Cowboy Poet

Baxter Black and gave him a large smattering of new poems. He replied:

> *"Whit, master of the salt lick and twisted hyperbole, poet whose verse is to be shaken and not stirred, and author of Lapses in Synapses, deserves to be exposed to an equal intellect outcast. Einstein meeting Helen Keller, Churchill meeting the Unabomber or an attention-deficit chimpanzee meeting a studious orangutan."*

I'm still not certain what that all means, but I think it's good. In any case, thanks Baxter.

Creating, metered rhythmed and rhymed 'nonsense' verse is an engaging word puzzle. It is a form of music, where mere words create the tune and where in its defining, cleverness and brevity live harmoniously in the same poem.

Rhymed poetry is also an addiction which this book is a product of. I am not addicted to drugs or alcohol or such: I am addicted to words and wordplay. The poetry in this book was written not as a distraction from life, nor a reflection of it. It was written to fill up waking hours of insomnia and boredom during rest-less times of travel, waiting for appointments or to catch a flight or a train, times when normal people are too nervous to read and instead pit their brains to ponder crosswords or sudokus.

My habit evolved from various enablers: Hink Pink, reading Ogden Nash, reading Walt Kelly, my dad reciting poetry in the bathtub, and a love of Limericks--both funny and clean. The poems here come from more years than I wish to admit.

Whit

FOREWORD

A discussion brews over the status of rhyming poetry. Some non-rhymers tend to look down on rhymed poetry as a gimmick or kid's stuff as in nursery rhymes (forgetting that they were political and an ingenious and an anonymous way to make fun of a government). These non-rhymers are intolerant and I am intolerant of such people.

Recently there have been newer discoveries of older editions of the Dead Sea Scrolls. What they have yielded so far has been astonishing and if rumor is correct, they contain Eve's memoir, *Vipers! My Asp!* Unabashed and unauthorized interpretation of this discovery is debatable, but apparently, she begins her book: *In the beginning* (How else could she have started it?) and from there explains what life was like revealing how Adam began changing his grunts into blowing raspberries mimicking Eve's farts. If this is true, then not only would this have been rhyming poetry's kick start, it would have marked the start of language as well. It would also be the first recorded incident of original humor.

What, you might ask, does this have to do with the book you are currently holding? Well, it is at this point, this farting leading to raspberries leading to man's first meaningful grunts; the genesis of language is rarely used as a format in poetry. And yet this rhyming process best fits and categorizes Whit's poetry. As primitive as these poems are, no one has filled this gap like Whit.

And, when it comes to Whit's work, describing it as "Poetry" and "poems" should be taken in the broadest sense of the words because his modus operandi was to scribble illegible notes on the backs of lotto tickets, parking tickets, traffic violations and unpaid bills. These he kept in a large paper bag and on occasion would shake the bag and extract his notes until several shared the same ideas—or didn't. Not exactly genius but dangerously interesting. These are his "poems."

Bill Harzia
Freeloadia, August 2021

WHAT ON EARTH?

When Atlas lifted the world
People were astounded
When they asked him what he stood on
Atlas was confounded

OVER UNDER INSIDE OUT

(It still doesn't fit)

The hospital gown
Makes Greek statues frown
You see it in their sculpted faces
And they say in disgust
That always they will trust
The fig leaf the gown replaces

I'LL TAKE A DOZEN

Roses are red
Violets are blue
Unless you're color blind
Then it's all brown to you

A BLACK DAY IN THE BLACK FOREST

Hansel and Gretel
Listened to heavy metal
When they lost their way

The Witch, she liked Beethoven
When she cooked them in the oh-ven
Tasty fat morsels were they

WE WILL ROCK YOU

Growing older
Pushing his boulder
Sisyphus retired to the valley
And there he yearned
To be the ball return
In the bowling alley

MEDUSA GOES TO IRELAND

Medusa had green snakes for hair
For what, no one recalled
She sailed and saw Saint Patrick
And now she's gone quite bald

RAPUNZEL

Rapunzel, Rapunzel
Pulled up her long long hair
She put it up in curlers
The boys now use the stairs

RAPUNZEL, THE SEQUEL

Strange affairs in her tower
Her hair did allow her
But no longer does her hair cater
She's put in an elevator

NO PLACE LIKE DOME

An avid leg puller
Was Buckminster Fuller
Regarding geodesic domes
He told Jack Horner
To sit in the corner
In circles Jack still roams

LITTLE JACK R.I.P.

Little Jack Horner
Was sent to the coroner
Obviously strangled to death
But the coroner with his thumb
From Jack's mouth pulled a plum
And said, "T'was this which robbed him of breath"

WHERE DO THEY COME FROM?

Little Jack Horner
Sat in the corner
Watching the dust bunnies play

Then with one quick maneuver
He pulled out his Hoover
And sucked them all away

CHRISTMAS IN HAWAII

We three tourists disoriented are
Just got the keys to our rental car
They said they wouldn't mind it
If we could go find it
They said it wasn't that far

Oh oh, which car is it?
Which car is right?
Did they say blue?
I thought they said white

We think we now just found our car
One of a million we had to look far
The keys they fit
So this must be it
Who's that following us, is that a police car?

Oh oh, these new cars
They all look the same
Have they copied each other?
Or am I going insane?

We three tourists arrested we are
We got pulled over, we didn't get far
It was all accidental
It wasn't our rental
We have been charged with stealing a car

Oh oh which brand was it
if we only knew
Was a Ford or Chevy
A Subaru?

We three tourists in jail we are
All because we took the wrong car
These judicial proceedings
Sure are misleading
It's Christmas in Hawaii spent behind bars

JOB DESCRIPTION: SHEEP RUSTLER

Mary had a little lamb
She stole it from Bo Peep
Along came the brand inspector
Now she's in trouble deep

J & J GO TO C

Jack and Jill went to sea
In a beautiful pea green boat
But Jack fell in and couldn't swim
And Jill? She died of laughter

THE UNINSURABLE JACK AND JILL

Jack and Jill
Took to the hills
For bottled water they yearned
But Jill she stumbled
Making Jack tumble
Oh, when are they going to learn?

BECAUSE IT WAS THERE

Jack and Jill took to climbing
This time neither fell
But unlucky was their timing
For an avalanche swept them to
Where they were never heard of or seen again

WHO GOT TO FIRST FIRST?

T'was at last to be settled; the final great debate
Humpty, he came early; the chicken he was late

LITTLE MISS MUFFIT

Little Miss Muffit
Sat on a tuffit*
Eating Mother Goose
Along came the Spider Man
And sat down beside her and
Slurped up all the juice

    *There were no chairs.

2 UNFINISHED

There was an old lady who lived in a shoe
She had athletes' foot; her kids did too...

*

The Owl and the Pussycat went to see
An LGBTQ attorney...

UNTIDALED

Blind with emotion
She went to the ocean
Where the cliffs are extremely steep
And there she wept
Then finally leapt
At the place called Lover's Leap

But while doing her pouting
The tide took to outing
And the tour guides now show
Where lost love and gravity
Made a large cavity
Way down on the beach below

A MATHMATICAL FANATICAL

Even the hypotenuse
Is of little use
Vying for persuasion
For in love's triangling
There is no untangling
This impossible equation

AT A MEGALOMANIAC CONVENTION

At a megalomaniac convention
I fell in love with me
So, I proposed to myself and asked,
Will you marry me?

No, I said, I'm too good for you!
Yet much to my chagrin
No, was not an answer
So, I asked myself again

Please marry me I asked once more
The question now redundant
But when your ego is big like mine
Results are not abundant

I went to the county courthouse
For a license to see me through
All they did was look at me
And said, there's only one of you!

I then went home to kill myself
But I'd had my run of luck
For every time I shot myself
My ego made me duck

And now here we all sit
The two of us that's me
Blaming megalomania
For my split personality

A BURNING DESIRE

He was an arsonist
And a narcissist
Who got burnt by his own desire
For he was cremated
By the love he created
Setting his heart on fire

ONLY THE LONELY

On love alone the narcissist dieted
He starved to death; a love unrequited

AN EXISTENTIALIST'S DILEMMA

My psychosomatic girlfriend
Catches my sicknesses too
But she can't really catch them
Because I'm psychosomatic too

My psychosomatic girlfriend
Faked her death today
I knew she was faking it
But I buried her anyway

My girlfriend's condition is factitious
But it comes with a twist
it makes me rather suspicious
Because she doesn't exist

VINI VIDI DA VINCI

Tell me, tell me, Mona Leeze
What's that expression you wear with ease?

I'm begging to know; I'm on my knees,
If you'd only tell me, won't you please!

Is your mouth glued shut with Mozzarella cheese?
Or is it filled with a thousand-and-one peas?

Do you have a case of fleas?
Are you chilled by a winter breeze?

Maybe you're about to sneeze!
I'll bet you drank some antifreeze!

So please won't you tell me Mona Leeze
What's that expression you wear with such ease?

SEASONED GREETINGS

Standing on a sage
Not wearing any cloves
Aren't you rather chili?
Only oreganos

Too many seasons in a year
Is that the way it goes?
Does thyme hold you at bay
Only oreganos

THANKS A LOT, LOT

It wasn't the wife's fault
She got rendered into salt
Yet what the Bible won't tell us
Is why Lot gets so jealous

Witnessed a nearby cow
"That's really some know how
The apex of all tricks
Turning humans to salt licks"

CANNIBALISING POE

It wasn't the love
He was thinking of
But into love fell he
For he went missing
When last seen kissing
His lovely Cannibal Lee

MEN'S LIVES

If it's the lives of men
Not fish we buy
Aren't then
Cannibals you and I?

A NORTH BEACH DIET

Jack Sprat could eat no fat
Anorexic was his wife
One day Jack got hungry
Now he's doing life

SIMPLY SIMON

Simple Simon
Met a cannibal
Going to the fair

He never made it

SIMPLE SIMON MEETS ALBERT

Simple Simon met Albert Einstein
Pondering unawares
Said Einstein to the Simon
$E=MC^2$

SIMPLE SIMON NEVER ENDS

Simple Simon met a Pi man
A numerical nightmare was he
Said Pi man to the Simon
I end in infinity

SIMPLE SIMON NEVER GETS THERE

Simple Simon used a GPS
To help him find the fair
But the coordinates lied
When the batteries died
Oh, where is Simon, oh where?

2B OR NOT 2B

Once I was proud, yellow and tall
But as I got older, I grew small

Now what I have is all that I've got
Soon I'll be sharpened until I am not

My life as a pencil seems such a waste
For all that I write is quickly erased

So, it's ashes to ashes, shavings to shavings
My point of view is really not worth saving

But life in the trash will be nothing new
Just a place to be buried, a room with no view

POETRY IN MOTION

In Pisa there is a tower
That leans more by the hour
I hope this leaning ceases
Or it'll be the leaning tower of

Pieces

FLEE FLY FLOW FLUNG

To Ben Mcduff poor Mary would cling
When Ben McDuff did his highland fling
But so fast did he fling that she came unclung
And over Scottish Highlands she was flung

DIPPED STRIPPED AND SHIPPED

Clasp unclipped
The flop it flipped
The script it was passed over
The French dipped
Stiff upper lipped
A courtship thus left over
The pink slipped
The blue chipped
The sponsorship once over
The weather stripped
The skinny dipped
The day tripped on hungover
Then pistol whipped
The Censor shipped
Until finally, Q tipped on over

DOUBTING THOMAS

Thomas Doubting did what Doubting Thomas's do
He doubted he existed, he doubted if he was true
"I am! Therefore, I doubt," said our doubting Tom
I doubt I had any parents, a dad or loving mom
He doubted all there was to doubt, he even doubted doubt
He doubted he was living life; he was doubt devout
He doubted he could hang himself, he doubted his demise
Thomas Doubting went to his grave, a surprised look in his eyes

MODEL Y

Henry Ford went to town
Feeling autographic
Wrote his name upon a car
And called it auto traffic

BEASTS OF WORDIN'

NOT SEAGULL! I SAID BEAGLE*

Charles Darwin fled from town
Feeling less than regal
For in his notes he resolved
He'd descended from a Beagle*

*HMS

THE NOTORIOUS PIG
(BY ANONYMOUSLY BIG)

This is the tale of a fat little piggy
Pursued relentlessly by a wolf named Iggy
Not one of those who huffed and puffed
Of which I know you've heard more than enough
This Iggy was different, this Iggy was strange
Iggy wanted Piggy cooked at his home with a range
For Iggy was evil, Iggy was bad
Chasing our doomed Piggy with all that he had
He chased poor Piggy near and far
He chased him with planes, he chased him with cars
From mountain passes down to the sea
Iggy refused to let our fat Piggy be...
Then one day he cornered Piggy on the edge of a cliff
And Piggy thought hard, he thought...what if?
What if... it's true that pigs can fly
I think it's a good time to give it a try
Piggy musters all the courage he's got
But Iggy the wolf is reading his thoughts
Says Iggy to piggy "Newton's laws are true
Don't think they don't apply to you
Besides you're a loser, not a winner

You've been consigned to be my dinner!
So now I suggest, get ready to die"
Said Piggy to Iggy, "In a wolf's eye"
And just when Iggy thought of eating roast pig rump
Was the very moment that piggy did jump
Iggy watched with hungry despair
His dinner escape at 32 feet per second squared
However, Piggy, himself, feeling it breezy
Mistakenly thought that this flying was easy!
So happy was Piggy that he began squealing
Leaving Iggy behind, starving and reeling
So here is our pig reaching terminal velocity
You've got to admit it a unique curiosity

When suddenly Piggy realized he was free fallin'
Piggy stopped squealing; and started a squallin'
For indeed there was no denying
Falling and flailing: This was not flying
Piggy shouted, Curse you, Isaac Newton!
Did your apples ever think of parachutin'?
Then Piggy thought "What a horrible way
To know F really does equal M x A!"
Meaning velocity, pig, and gravity
Were about to make a large cavity
Reuniting back with planet Earth
But I'll tell you this, for what it's worth
For I know you think it is here piggy dies
That pigs never did, and never will fly
This is sure; this is for certain
That Piggy's time is up; it looks like pig curtains
But it's here our tale goes amuck
For piggy is brokered a small piece of luck
That is, Piggy's fall is completely broken
By powers that remain mostly unspoken
Which is how Piggy escaped Iggy the wolf
Softly landing upon an abattoir's roof
And so ends our tale, the strange mystery
Of the pig that made sausage ...but not, history

THE COYOTE

The coyote he
Howls because of his fleas
The coyote she
Howls along in harmonies

THE KOALA

With teeth the Almighty's equipped us
To chew on this eucalyptus
Else we'd be here to kingdom come
Chewing upon this gum tree gum

THE HIPPOPOTOMOUSE

A rare and dangerous species
is the hippopotomouse
If you get one in your attic
Then you'd better leave your house

BOVINE HEAVEN

Once I drove through Tennessee
A place I did not wish to be
For it was dark I could not see
The cow in the road in front of me
But there she stood in the middle of the road
I was going too fast when I should have slowed
So, as it happened, I did plow
Up the rear end of that cow
When the ambulance did arrive
I heard them say the cow had died
But what they said next was very queer
That the driver of the car had disappeared
I tried to yell I tried to shout
Yet not a sound did come out
Then the police came and looked around
But no trace of me could be found
They looked for me most everywhere
Except up in that cow's derriere
So, there I was trapped and vexed
Wondering what would happen next
When heavenly bound we did transcend
That cow, with me stuck in its rear end
Now Jonah may have lived in a whale's gut
But he didn't go to heaven in a bovine's butt
Well, we arrived at a golden cattle grate
A place where I was to await my fate
The man at the grate said his name was Kevin
And welcomed me to bovine heaven
He told me I could come out now
That I did not have to hide inside a cow
I looked around and I'll tell you this

This wasn't a place of heavenly bliss
There were no fluffy clouds, no RIP
...At least I wasn't left in Tennessee
But in cow heaven eternity is a disaster
You see cow years pass 5 to 1 faster
Its forever and a day with what to do?
Won't someone please light the barbeque?

MY DOG FIDO

My poor Dog Fido
Swallowed some pie dough
But the dough was loaded
And poor Fido exploded
(I really don't know why though)

FLATTERY WILL GET YOU NO WHERE

NOT A DOUBLE CROSSER

Looking out through masked eyes
Thinking he was in disguise
Regrettably he failed to see
That he was crossing State Route 3
Caught in the headlights he went splat
And that's how I got my coon skin hat

CROWING IN B FLAT

The Rooster crowed
As he crossed the road
A very brave rooster was he
But the road was wide
And the other side
Was impossible to see
His stride it slowed
While the crowing he crowed
Began to sound off key
Then out ran his luck
When along came a truck
Now his crowing is flat as can be

MY TOM CAT TOM

My Tom Cat Tom
Now sings the 33rd Psalm
For although curiosity kills the cat
T'was the Fed-Ex truck that squished Tom flat

THE RACCOON

He's called a bandit
And it isn't so
Yet why are his eyes masked?
You ask
Surely, he must know

MANE THAT TUNE

The lion's biggest problem
Is mainly when he snores
Even when he's sleeping
He does so with a roar

THE RABACOON

With a shuffling sound
The zookeeper found
A scene not of natural selection
There was a baboon
Embraced with a raccoon
Who was wearing no protection

On an October morn
The baby was born
The controversy started sooner than later
It didn't look like a racoon
Or a baboon
But it did look like the zoo's curator

PONCE DE LEON

So strong was the effervescence
It turned his men into adolescents
Boyish pranks his men imparted
They snickered and giggled when they farted
Seeing his men act so uncouth
Ponce thought: This was no Fountain of Youth
With its vast array of impurities
This is the Spring of Immaturities
Yet the future Ponce failed to see
What this spring would turn out to be
For when the press uncovered
What Ponce discovered
The land developers charged in
And much to Ponce's chagrin
Bought up all the lando
Of what Is now Orlando
For this Ponce's life unfurled
And what do we get: Disney World

ONCE THE GARDEN OF EDEN: NOW A TOXIC WASTE SITE

This is where an orchard once grew
Yellow Delicious, Rayburn and, Honeydew
No longer do they exist
Galas, Macintosh or, Granny Smiths

A RENTAL AGREEMENT GONE AWRY

From a tree the words hissed,
"Hey human! Get a load of this!"
And then: "You don't have to be suspicious
"For apples are riper
"When polished by a viper
"Go on! It's a red delicious!"

Resisting all but the temptational
Eve claimed the apple sensational
Then a voice from the sky boomed, "Sinner! Atone!
"This is red-code alarming
"That you find the devil charming
"And to think this is an apple-free zone!"

And so, Adam and Eve
Were given permanent leave
For eating the fruit that was restricted
God was so galled
The sheriff he called
And had the couple evicted

THE CENTIPEDE

How do you make your legs agree?
Which way you're going to proceed?
Which legs do you make follow?
Which legs do you make lead?
Isn't it a problem, running at full speed?
Good golly Moses, centipede
Just one of you makes a stampede!

THE RATTLE SNAKE

The rattle is maybe
Because he's part baby
But check his diaper
You'll see he's a viper

PASSIONATE GROANS AND BROKEN BONES

When the python falls in love
He does so with a crush
Not the way you're thinking of
But still, it'd make you blush

THE VULTURE

The vulture won't hurt you
His patience is virtue
He'll just wait till you're dead
So, he can be fed

IT'S EIDER DOWN OR UP: THE GOOSES'S LAMENT

I can't go up you stole my down
And left me stuck here on the ground
With all you took I don't know why
Your sleeping bag should surely fly

SWIM SWAM SWAN
(A SWAN SONG GONE WRONG)

singing that song
of a bing gone bong
a ring that once rang
a rung all wrong

a flea that's flung
a cling comes unclung
slang becomes slung
with the slip of a tongue

like a king missing kong
a ding without dong
where hangnails are hung
the swan's song is sung

THE LEMMING

The lemming's way
Is like Hemingway's

TO BEE OR NOT TO BEE

The because is the pollen
The bee buzz is the haulin'

BYE BYE BA BA

Ba Ba Black sheep have you any wool?

Ba yourself, said the sheep, do think I'm a fool?
Pray tell, what from a sheep do you think you obtain
The wool business I'm in and in it I shall remain
A senseless question, asking me for wool!
Why sir! Three bags of it you're full!

The farmer turned red as he lost his cool
No longer did he want a thread of wool
That sheep coat the farmer did unbutton
Revealing beneath a feast of mutton

MERMAID

If you were made
Full of sexual wishes
Would you still choose the half?
to accommodate the fishes?

THE WOOD PECKER

With all that pecking
You are certainly wrecking
All that is tranquil
And the pills you must take
To ease your headache
Who pays your aspirin bill?

BLIND LOVE

it is not a porcupine's practice
to fall in love with a cactus
but this one was blind
and quickly did he find
true love
and that is what the fact is

PORCUPINES

Pet porcupines require love
But always pet them with a glove

LINGERING LING COD

Grasped in the fish monger's fingers
The lingering ling cod now lingers
For in the fingers of the fish monger
A ling cod will linger no longer

SEEDING CLOUDS

A giraffe's head is so high it
Lets them eat clouds for a diet
But in skies where there are few clouds
Eating clouds is not allowed
Science shows there's little doubt
That eating clouds causes drought
But the giraffe just eats and laughs and laughs
Because that's the modality of giraffes
Eating clouds is a must
Cirrus, Stratus, and Cumulus
And so, they eat the clouds they need
Carefully spitting out the seeds

LOUIE (FORMALLY FROM LIHUI)

This Is the tale of powder monkey Louie
His behavior suspect, his practices screwy
For Louie wasn't one to let things be
He set off on a dynamiting spree
People began to wonder why
People like the F.B.I.
Who didn't care and hardly did notice
Until he dynamited out one lousy POTUS
Louie started young, he started small
By blowing up his brother Paul
When his teachers said he's got ADHD
He answered them with TNT
When his parents found what he had done
He blew them both to Kingdom Come
He dynamited all things of creation
Like the probing police he'd locked in their station
(For effect he packed in lots of powder
Just to make the explosion louder)
But Louie never did get caught
The hunt for him was all for naught
Because one day he used
A far too short, length of fuse
Well, nothing is wronger
Than a fuse that should've been longer
On top of this, and just for fun
He lit the fuse, but didn't run...

And...

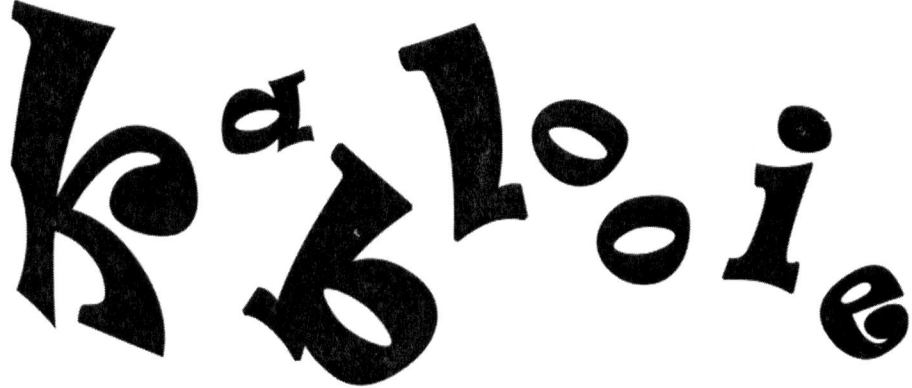

Went Louie...
It was a spectacular ascent
Everywhere that Louie went
It rained Louie all over the place
But much of him joined outer space
Like, what used to be his fatty girth?
Now daily, orbits round the earth
Yet other parts of Louie were found
Way up there around Puget Sound
Louis' end though was a bit dreary
Not half as big as the Big Bang Theory
Louie got around; his presence vast
In fact, most say, he was a blast
Today, although bits of Louie ride solar winds
It is here on earth where this tale and book now ends.